The Glittering World of Gems

INCREDIBLE EMERALDS

By Amy B. Rogers

KidHaven
PUBLISHING

Published in 2018 by
KidHaven Publishing, an Imprint of Greenhaven Publishing, LLC
353 3rd Avenue
Suite 255
New York, NY 10010

Designer: Seth Hughes
Editor: Vanessa Oswald

Photo credits: Cover (left) Muellek Josef/Shutterstock.com; cover (right) TinaImages/Shutterstock.com; cover, pp. 1–2, 4, 6, 8, 10, 12, 14, 16, 18, 20–21, back cover (background) ILeysen/Shutterstock.com; p. 5 murboy/Getty Images; p. 7 Sviatoslav Mishin/Shutterstock.com; p. 9 Victor Moussa/Shutterstock.com; pp. 11, 13 Alejandra Parra/Bloomberg via Getty Images; pp. 12, 17 Jan Sochor/Latincontent/Getty Images; p. 15 Reimphoto/Thinkstock; p. 19 Cheshmeh Studio/Shutterstock.com; p. 20 (top) Rob Stothard/Getty Images; p. 20 (bottom) ADRIAN DENNIS/AFP/Getty Images; p. 21 (top) Everett Collection/Shutterstock.com; p. 21 (bottom) Ra'ike/Wikimedia Commons.

Cataloging-in-Publication Data

Names: Rogers, Amy B.
Title: Incredible emeralds / Amy B. Rogers.
Description: New York : KidHaven Publishing, 2018. | Series: The glittering world of gems | Includes index.
Identifiers: ISBN 9781534523135 (pbk.) | 9781534523067 (library bound) | ISBN 9781534522961 (6 pack) | ISBN 9781534523036 (ebook)
Subjects: LCSH: Emeralds–Juvenile literature. | Mineralogy–Juvenile literature.
Classification: LCC QE394.E5 R64 2018 | DDC 553.8'6–dc23

Printed in the United States of America

CPSIA compliance information: Batch #BS17KL: For further information contact Greenhaven Publishing LLC, New York, New York at 1-844-317-7404.

Please visit our website, www.greenhavenpublishing.com. For a free color catalog of all our high-quality books, call toll free 1-844-317-7404 or fax 1-844-317-7405.

CONTENTS

HOW EMERALDS ARE MADE

Emeralds are bright green gems. They form deep inside the earth when hot **magma** cools. These **transparent** crystals are made of the **mineral** beryl. This mineral is generally clear and almost colorless.

The reason emeralds are green is because beryl mixes with the element chromium as it cools. It takes millions of years for emerald crystals to form.

Mining for Facts!

The first emerald mines existed in Egypt more than 5,000 years ago.

Emeralds are used in all kinds of **jewelry.**

MINES FULL OF EMERALDS

Today, the most popular country to find emeralds is Colombia in South America. The Colombian cities of Muzo and Chivor have emerald mines that are hundreds of years old. The Inca peoples found emerald **deposits** there before the Spanish settled in the area. Once the Spanish arrived, they used the Incas as slaves to dig more tunnels because they wanted more emeralds.

The Colombian mines still produce many gem-**quality** stones each year. Brazil and Zambia are the other two major countries where emeralds are mined.

Mining for Facts!

Emeralds have also been found in Pakistan, Russia, Afghanistan, Canada, Australia, and the United States.

Raw emeralds form in rocks in places such as Colombia or Brazil.

DIFFERENT SHADES OF EMERALD

Emeralds of the highest value are a deep green that looks like the color of grass and are very clear. However, emeralds come in different shades of green.

As these six-sided crystals form deep inside the earth, other minerals can get trapped inside them. This can change an emerald's color. Bubbles of gas or liquid can also get trapped in the crystals, creating a flaw or inclusion. These can make emeralds appear cloudy and lower their value.

Mining for Facts!

Beryl is made up of many elements, including beryllium, aluminum, and silicon. Different kinds of beryl are different colors.

Emeralds that are blue-green or pure green have the highest value.

THE LIFE OF AN EMERALD MINER

Emerald mining is very hard work and can be unsafe. Miners dig deep tunnels to pull the emeralds out of the ground. They use hand tools to dig through the rocks and dirt, which are then brought to the surface in hand carts. The rocks are washed by miners hoping to discover emeralds.

Emerald miners only mine by hand and don't use machines because the machines could destroy the emeralds. It's easy to break emeralds because they can be hard to see in the mine and trapped in other rocks.

Mining for Facts!

The best emeralds are found closest to the earth's surface.

Shown here is a miner in Colombia pushing a cart of rocks and dirt out of an emerald mine.

MINING IN AN OPEN PIT

The most common way to search for emeralds is open-pit mining. Miners make the opening wider at the top, and the hole gets narrower toward the bottom of the mine. Miners often work on small pieces of land close to one another.

Once the miners dig out a small amount of rocks and dirt, they carefully wash it. Since this kind of mining needs a lot of water, open-pit mines are generally located near large sources of water.

Emerald miners are shown here digging in an open-pit mine in Muzo, Colombia.

CREATING EMERALD JEWELRY

When raw emeralds are ready to be made into jewelry, they are sent to a **lapidary**. Gem-quality crystals are cut and **polished** by the lapidary before being placed into a piece of jewelry.

The lapidary cuts the emerald crystal away from the rock it's found in with a diamond saw. An emerald is a very hard stone. However, it can be split easily where it has inclusions. The lapidary works very slowly to make sure they don't damage the stone or cut away **valuable** crystal. Once an emerald is taken out of the rock, it's ready to be shaped.

Mining for Facts!

The larger a jeweler makes an emerald, the more valuable it is.

These are shiny, gem-quality emeralds.

ADDING FACETS TO AN EMERALD

Once lapidaries have removed the raw emeralds from rocks, they add **facets** to them. This gives the gems a finished look and makes them shine under light. To add facets, a lapidary holds the emerald on a stick with wax. This stick allows the lapidary to place the emerald against a **grinding wheel**. These facets need to be evenly placed for the emerald to be valuable.

Emeralds are generally cut into what's called an emerald cut. This means the emerald is shaped into a square or a rectangle. Jewelers say this shape shows off the color and shine of an emerald best.

Shown here is a lapidary grinding facets into an emerald crystal.

AN EMERALD'S VALUE

The most important qualities that make an emerald valuable are its cut, color, and **clarity**. Jewelers call emeralds with evenly spaced facets "Greenfire" because of their bright color. These emeralds are the shiniest.

Emeralds without any flaws are the most expensive gems in the world. These gems often have a higher level of clarity than other gems. Emeralds are more valuable than diamonds of the same weight. All gems are measured in a unit called the carat. Five carats are equal to 0.035 ounce (1 g).

These gems are shaped into an emerald cut that makes them very shiny and colorful.

FAMOUS EMERALDS

What: Elizabeth Taylor's emerald and diamond necklace

When: made in 1962

Where: purchased in Italy by Richard Burton, who became her husband

Weight: 60.5 carats (12.1 g)

Value: more than $12 million

What: German Prince Guido Henckel von Donnersmarck's emerald and diamond tiara

When: The German prince gave his second wife the tiara in 1900.

Where: emeralds came from Colombia

Weight: 500 carats (100 g)

Value: $13 million

What: Angelina Jolie's emerald earrings

When: 2009

Where: worn to the Academy Awards in California

Weight: 115 carats (23 g)

Value: $2.5 million

What: Hooker Emerald Brooch

When: Jewelry company Tiffany & Co. purchased the emerald in 1911 and put it in a tiara. In 1950, the gem was put in a brooch. In 1955, the brooch was purchased by Janet Annenberg Hooker, who the emerald is named after.

Where: It was first taken from a mine in Colombia in the 16th or 17th century. It has been at the Smithsonian Institution since 1977.

Weight: 75 carats (15 g)

Value: $500,000

GLOSSARY

clarity: The state of being clear.

deposit: An amount of a mineral in the ground that built up over a period of time.

facet: Flat sides that are cut into a gem.

grinding wheel: A wheel used to shape or smooth something with a rough surface.

jewelry: Pieces of metal, often holding gems, that are worn on the body.

lapidary: A person who cuts and polishes gems to be used for jewelry.

magma: Hot, liquid rock deep inside the earth.

mineral: A natural, solid substance that is not a plant or animal.

polish: To rub something with a soft cloth to make it smooth and shiny.

quality: The standard of something.

transparent: Easily seen through.

valuable: Of great worth.

FOR MORE INFORMATION

Websites

Gem Kids: Emeralds
gemkids.gia.edu/gem/emerald
This website includes colorful pictures and fun facts about emeralds.

National Geographic Kids: Emerald
kids.nationalgeographic.com/explore/science/emerald/#emerald-raw.jpg
This website has cool illustrations and interesting information about emeralds.

Books

Farndon, John. *Rocks, Minerals and Gems*. Richmond Hill, ON: Firefly Books, 2016.

VanVoorst, Jenny Fretland. *Gems*. Minneapolis, MN: Core Library, 2015.

Publisher's note to educators and parents: Our editors have carefully reviewed these websites to ensure that they are suitable for students. Many websites change frequently, however, and we cannot guarantee that a site's future contents will continue to meet our high standards of quality and educational value. Be advised that students should be closely supervised whenever they access the Internet.

INDEX